Cornwall
Edited by Jessica Woodbridge

Young**Writers**

First published in Great Britain in 2005 by:
Young Writers
Remus House
Coltsfoot Drive
Peterborough
PE2 9JX
Telephone: 01733 890066
Website: www.youngwriters.co.uk

All Rights Reserved

© Copyright Contributors 2005

SB ISBN 1 84602 134 0

Foreword

Young Writers was established in 1991 and has been passionately devoted to the promotion of reading and writing in children and young adults ever since. The quest continues today. Young Writers remains as committed to the fostering of burgeoning poetic and literary talent as ever.

This year's Young Writers competition has proven as vibrant and dynamic as ever and we are delighted to present a showcase of the best poetry from across the UK. Each poem has been carefully selected from a wealth of *Playground Poets* entries before ultimately being published in this, our thirteenth primary school poetry series.

Once again, we have been supremely impressed by the overall high quality of the entries we have received. The imagination, energy and creativity which has gone into each young writer's entry made choosing the best poems a challenging and often difficult but ultimately hugely rewarding task - the general high standard of the work submitted amply vindicating this opportunity to bring their poetry to a larger appreciative audience.

We sincerely hope you are pleased with our final selection and that you will enjoy *Playground Poets Cornwall* for many years to come.

Contents

Richard Creber (11) — 1
Olivia Grant (11) — 2

Darite Primary School
Karl Daniels (10) — 3
Jordan Dennis (9) — 4
Daniel Bolitho (11) — 5
David Ward (11) — 6
Emily Jenkins (10) — 7
Oliver Jenkins (10) — 8
Charis Ward (10) — 9
Corrie McDonald (10) — 10
Lucy Hillman (10) — 11
Holly Thorne (10) — 12
Louise Sexton (10) — 13
Rosie Meitiner (9) — 14
Andrew Brown (10) — 15
Alyce Martini-Richards (10) — 16
Dylan Peel (10) — 17
Piers Loughrey-Robinson (9) — 18
Oliver Gunning (10) — 19
Beth Ridley (10) — 20
Lauren Hedley (8) — 21
Courtney Sexton (7) — 22
Gemma Wilkinson (7) — 23
Sammy Vine (8) — 24
Chloe Gunning (8) — 25
Luca Martini (8) — 26
Tristan Loughrey-Robinson (7) — 27
Alex Sawley (8) — 28
Leeza Hodge (8) — 29
Ben Ackland (8) — 30
Nathaniel Vine (9) — 31
Luke Payne (9) — 32
Aaron Sexton (8) — 33
Luke Serpell (9) — 34
Barrie-Jon Hutton (8) — 35
Rebecca Ferguson (9) — 36
Tilly Dimond (9) — 37

Grampound-With-Creed CE School
Rae Langton (11) — 38
Lucy Pearce (8) — 39
Declan Byrne (10) — 40
Sophie Bourne (8) — 41
Niamh Byrne (7) — 42
Ciara Langton (7) — 43
Dan Ford (10) — 44
Kester Westbrook Netherton (8) — 45
Ben Howe (7) — 46
Jack Nelson (10) — 47
Anna Venning (8) — 48
Jasmine Tse (10) — 49
Charlotte Juleff (11) — 50
Edward Tse (9) — 51
Lucinda Thayers (7) — 52
Shane Williams (10) — 53
Sasha Fann (8) — 54
Lucas Swain (9) — 55
Eva Saul (8) — 56
Jordan Still (8) — 57
Keziah Davies (9) — 58

Launceston CP School
Aidan Whale (9) — 59
Abigail Cleave (9) — 60
William De Ferrars (9) — 61
Cathryn Cruickshank (10) — 62
Bradley Cameron (9) — 63
Tyler Brooker (9) — 64
Adam Matthews (10) — 65
Chantelle Oldaker (9) — 66
Joshua McCabe (10) — 67
Tom Ellacott (10) — 68
Bethany Addicott (9) — 69
William Vanstone (10) — 70
Richard Burdon (10) — 71
Hannah Perkins (9) — 72
Abigael Stevenson (10) — 73
Joy Gibbs (7) — 74

Kimberly Thomas (8)	75
Megan Vanstone (7)	76
Tristan Parsons (7)	77
Jack Hogan (8)	78
James Cleave (7)	79
Sebastian Fletcher (8)	80
Josie Stevenson (7)	81
Anne Mallett (8)	82
Naomi Choak (8)	83
Henry Williams (8)	84
Marcus Hill (8)	85
Thomas Gist (8)	86
Rebecca Vidler (7)	87
Kayleigh Jenkins (8)	88
Lewis Matthews (8)	89
Sophie Danson (7)	90
Jordan Karkeek (7)	91
Jessica Platt (7)	92
Cameron Hollidge (7)	93
Lucy Cameron (7)	94
Natalie Stevenson (8)	95
Robyn Land (9)	96
Bethany Chapman (8)	97
Abby Bounsall (9)	98
Alexander Shopland (8)	99
Claire Downing (9)	100
Laura Champ (8)	101
Liam Sloan (8)	102
Casey Nolan (9)	103
Charlotte Duff (8)	104
Megan Jackson (8)	105
Sophie Cameron (8)	106
Joshua Harris (9)	107
Elias O'Neill (8)	108
George Habgood (8)	109
Thomas Clogg (9)	110
Keziah Parnell (9)	111
Tobias Knights (8)	112
Thomas Davison (9)	113
Daniel Bradshaw (9)	114
Heather Davey (8)	115

Aron Finnimore (9)   116
Faron Tilley (8)   117
Zara Choak (10)   118
Mandy Sillifant (10)   119
Hannah Barnes (10)   120
William Samuels (11)   121
Duncan Whale (11)   122
Alexandra Wilton (10)   123
Robyn Wadman (10)   124
Harry Pooley (11)   125
Joshua Jackson (11)   126
Lewis Holden (10)   127
Lucy Perry (10)   128
Garod Gregory (9)   129

Luxulyan Primary School

Steven Hooper (11)   130
Simon Crocker (10)   131
Luke Rowe   132
Heather Charlesworth (11)   133
Nicola Smith (9)   134
Lauren Hoskin (10)   135
Benjamin Bond (9)   136
William George (11)   137
Millie Jones (10)   138
Jamie Jepson (11)   139
Josh Jepson (9)   140
Eddie Crocker (8)   141
Alex Nankivell (11)   142
Ashley Hick (10)   143
Eddie George (8)   144
Eve Pettican (7)   145
Samuel Hunt (8)   146

St Day & Carharrack Community School, Burnwithan

Jennifer Wade (10)   147
Hannah Bown (9)   148
Stephen Trenoweth (9)   149
Tyler Truman (9)   150
Sarah Collett (10)   151
Gillian Rapson (9)   152

The Poems

Adam M Jarvis (10)	189
Kenza Thompson-Hewitt (10)	190
Emily McConville (11)	191
Heidi Carthew (10)	192
Joseph Varker (10)	193

Werrington CP School

Katie Parkin (9)	194
Shannon Sargent (9)	195
Sam Wooldridge (9)	196
Danielle Stearn (9)	197
Alice Hopkins (8)	198
Mark Gribble (7)	199
Dean Parkin (7)	200
Harry Gilbert (8)	201

Samantha Dyer (9)   153
Julia Braddon (9)   154
Logan Reynolds (10)   155
Nessa Cawte (10)   156

St Mary's CE Primary School, Truro
Ellie Sayer (10)   157
Felicity Hamilton (10)   158
Harriet Skidmore (10)   159
Cara Loukes (10)   160
Tristan Latarche (10)   161
Hannah Cavill (9)   162
Hannah Vaughan (10)   163
Luke Dehaan (9)   164
Rhiannon Boon (9)   165
Jenna Maria Dingle (9)   166
Matthew Cook (10)   167
Thomas Bryant (10)   168
Elliot Powell   169
Holly Manley (9)   170
Lauren Jones (9)   171
Stephen Timms (9)   172
Joshua Collett (10)   173
Jake Rostill (9)   174
Aiden Franklin (9)   175
Isaac Sutcliffe (9)   176
Alexander Driver (10)   177
Rebecca Gorman (9)   178
Jacob De La Mare (10)   179
Lewis Jones (10)   180
William Perry (10)   181
Ross Whyte (10)   182
Courtney Rose Cavanagh (10)   183
Kai Hankins (9)   184

Threemilestone School
Shannon Bickham (10)   185
Odette Smaldon (11)   186
Elaine Dyer (11)   187
Laura Barr (11)   188

Countryside

Foragers are back in action for the harvest of the maize,
Tractors fired up for the pulling of the harvest home,
Finally, they're out in the fields bringing the golden cobs in,
The crop is safely gathered before the rain begins.

Shooters are getting their guns clean and ready,
Out in the woods and countryside the clays are flying high
And before you know, the year has turned and the harvest
                                              is home again.

Richard Creber (11)

Summing Up Summer

Daisies dotted to and fro,
The fresh breeze, let it blow,
Cheeping birds in the sky,
Elegant boats sail by.

The slight rustling of the trees,
The seagulls flutter about and will never cease,
Buttercups glow in the sun,
Children in the fields are having fun.

White horses jumping proud,
The houses surrounding me are playing music loud,
The mysterious fort sits upon the cliff,
I can smell the sea at Penlee, as I take a whiff.

Not to put pressure on you,
But somewhere in the sunny depths of Cornwall,
An unknown treasure
Has not been found,
And we want it to stay that way.

Olivia Grant (11)

All Around Me I See

All around me I see
The grass sitting looking at all its boring clones,
The trees looking like they have just been through a dirt wash,
The shed looking like it needs a face lift
And the concrete looking like stale bread.

All around me I see
Dull stones in a field,
Leaves getting tossed in the air from tree to tree,
The flowers feeling jealous and wanting to be colourful,
Weeds creeping up walls with nothing to look forward to.

All around me I see nothing but dullness.

Karl Daniels (10)
Darite Primary School

Who Cares?

Who cares about trees that are bare?
Who cares about twigs that are rotting?
Who cares about branches that are snapping off?
Who cares about trees that are left out in the cold?

The birds care!
The animals care!
The children care!
The teachers care!
In fact, everyone cares!

Jordan Dennis (9)
Darite Primary School

Unwanted

Scattered bins blowing away in the wind,
Temperature equipment left out,
Unused and uncared for.
A faded, brown, dirty shed
With a battered holey roof,
Padlocks on a rusty door,
That hasn't been opened in years.

A lifeless, leafless, bare dried out tree,
That has been chipped, kicked
And has rejected its leaves.
Overgrown grass taking control
And burying the still stone slabs,
Brown patches in the grass,
Which was once undisturbed
And crystal green.

A deserted wasteland of ground,
That looks identical to the bottom of the sea.
Moss growing out of the man-made walls and hedges,
Holes and thorns emerging from old worn out stones,
The end of something which was once magnificent.

Daniel Bolitho (11)
Darite Primary School

Could You Imagine?

Could you imagine?
Flowers, all pretty and broad amongst the grass,
Not mud, all dug up laying amongst broken glass.

Could you imagine?
A strong tree full of life amongst mushrooms in a bunch,
Not a couple of broken rocks amongst rubbish from a lunch.

Could you imagine?
A lively pond with a colourful lily,
Not lumps in the ground that are very hilly.

Of course you can't!
Because it's not true!
It hasn't yet happened!

David Ward (11)
Darite Primary School

Who Cares?

Who cares
About the lonely and bare trees?
Who cares
About the hard and abandoned rocks?
Who cares
About the lifeless weak plants?
The dull landscapes,
The mean and unfriendly crawling ivy
And the miserable shed staring right at you?
Who cares?
Who cares?

Who cares
About the long and forgotten leaves?
Who cares
About the neglected walls?
Who cares
About the unfriendly flowers blooming?
The abandoned and anxious mud just waiting for company
And the smelliest compost heap?
Who cares?
Who cares?

Emily Jenkins (10)
Darite Primary School

Who Cares?

Who cares
About the huge gloomy branches
Which help trees to produce new leaves?

Who cares
About the flowers
Which help produce more oxygen?

Who cares
About the flowers that have died
From trying to disperse new seeds?

Who cares
About the wavy grass
That is home to different insects?

Who cares
About the lonely shed
That has dull cobwebs hung around,
Like old Christmas decorations?

Who cares?
Who cares?

Oliver Jenkins (10)
Darite Primary School

Why Is the Landscape Playing Games?

The trees are playing musical statues,
The rocks are playing dead,
The grass is waving to me
And the air is playing catch round the flower bed.

Why is the landscape playing games?

The ivy is climbing, on the shed,
The floor is playing hide-and-seek
with the leaves and rubbish.
The trees are playing piggy-in-the-middle
with the wind,
The roots are swimming in the ground, like fish.

Why is the landscape playing games?

Because it's bored, because it's sad,
Because its good days have been had,
Because its life is now dead,
Because now it's time for it to be happy instead.

Charis Ward (10)
Darite Primary School

Today I Saw . . .

Today I saw . . .
A tree so bare, lonely and scared.
There, standing tall and interlocked with branches.
Grass that's plain, trodden on and ill treated,
Stones colourless, bland and boring.

Today I saw . . .
A flower longing to be beautifully colourful, like a butterfly,
Hoping to be red and green once again.
Walls kicked and battered,
Chipped and neglected.

Today I saw . . .
The shed bored from seeing no one
Apart from the little grass and bare trees.
A faded brown colour with holes all around.
Compost bins scattered.

Will anyone care for our poor old school?

Corrie McDonald (10)
Darite Primary School

Senses

Today I see . . .
The rough grimy mud covering the ground,
Wet tangled trees bare and lonely,
Dead twigs that have been lying there for years,
The dark misty skies there above me.

Today I feel . . .
The rain trickling past my face,
My feet sinking in mud as if it was gobbling me up,
The dull polluted wind blowing past me,
The cold uneven ground, freezing my feet.

Today I smell . . .
Damp deserted grass blown over by the wind,
Mouldy wood rotting away slowly,
The smoke billowing from chimneys,
The rosemary lying on the ground.

Today I see . . .
The ice cold trees, for they have no leaves,
Disordered stones scattered across the ground.
Ill-treated trees standing like statues.

The landscape deteriorating in front of me.

Lucy Hillman (10)
Darite Primary School

I Am Looking

I am looking at a giant tree,
Which once had humongous green leaves.
Then along came winter and swept them away
Like a dustpan and brush.
I am looking at that same old tree,
The one that had beautiful leaves.
Though now, it's all ugly and lonely,
The tree that looks like any other tree,
The tree that had beautiful leaves.

I am looking at a wall,
The wall that looks like you or me.
For the stones on the wall stand up
And down,
Reminding me
Of familiar faces.

I am looking at a landscape,
The landscape that stretches
For miles around.
I see the fields
Just sitting there,
Breathing in all of the calm air.

Soon all of these things will come to life,
Waking themselves from the long winter.

Holly Thorne (10)
Darite Primary School

The Lonely Tree

Today I see the lonely tree
Upon the slippery grass,
Waiting to see
The free flying bird,
Sitting upon his soggy leaves.

Today I see brown and grey leaves
Falling from the lonely tree.
The lonely tree wants to see
Happiness and to be free.

Today I see a lonely tree,
And beside that tree a rock,
That doesn't get to see
Grass that is green.

Louise Sexton (10)
Darite Primary School

Neglected

Hear the birds welcome you,
Feel the long neglected grass crawl up your leg,
See the damp bark flaking off the tree,
Smell the warm fires burning.

The winter leaves drifting by unnoticed.

Hear the overgrown grass squelch when you step on it.
Feel the chilly wind blowing against your face,
Smell the fresh pleasant air,
See our old, rusty, forgotten shed.
Neglected!

Rosie Meitiner (9)
Darite Primary School

The Lonely Old Corner

Who cares about the lonely old corner, deserted and bare
And the damp old tree by the soft compost heap?
The discoloured fence around,
The damp compost heap in the lonely old corner?

Who cares about the empty shed whose only friends are spiders,
In the unused field of overgrown grass,
That's as tall as a forest?
Under the shed whose friends are spiders,
Next to the discoloured fence,
Around the damp compost heap in the lonely old corner?

The only creatures that appear to care are:
The spiders,
The ants,
The beetles,
The flies
And the ladybirds.

But do they really care about
The damp compost heap in the lonely old corner?

Andrew Brown (10)
Darite Primary School

Our School Grounds

Trees, damp and dull,
Grass, wet and weary.
Rocks, dirty and destitute.
The ground, muddy and mossy,
Branches, spiky and scary,
The walls, bare and boring.
Fields frozen and flattened by the wind,
Imaginary flowers longing to grow
And glow with colour.

Alyce Martini-Richards (10)
Darite Primary School

Around Our School

The bare dull trees are longing to grow new leaves,
The discoloured walls doing nothing, day by day.
Blades of grass, waving in the wild, strong wind.
The deserted area of dead and lifeless weeds,
Saddens people who look upon it.

The boring, plain rocks unmoved
And watching everything around them.
By the brown uninteresting shed,
The small compost heap builds up,
Soon to be a large mud hill.
The undisturbed leaves are rotting every day
And the dead ivory stumps stay standing,
After years of rain and sunshine.

Clumps of mud pile onto the stony and grassy hedge,
The stone path is dirty due to muddy feet.
Strong gusts blow the twigs from tall trees,
Everything is waiting to come back to life.

Dylan Peel (10)
Darite Primary School

Deserted

Trees hoping for colour,
Stones hoping to see grass again.
Twigs hoping to be on trees,
Flowers hoping to be colourful,
Like the butterfly that flies overhead.

Walls hoping to stand and be seen,
Hedges hoping to be green.
A shed hoping to be used,
And a whole garden,
Hoping to grow beautifully.

Piers Loughrey-Robinson (9)
Darite Primary School

Ill-Treated

There you are
Standing in the middle of a field.
The only thing you look forward to
Is growing leaves.
You have been disrespected and ill-treated,
Every time something walks past
You are ignored.

There you are
You have been neglected and thrown,
You are abandoned and sad,
You are weak
And slowly but surely, chipping off.
When you look around you see
Plants, bright and beautiful,
All you ever wanted
Was to make yourself useful.
But instead,
You feel useless and ugly.

There you are,
You have been carelessly treated
By the wind.
All you see are other blades of grass.
All you ever wanted
Was to be different
And stand out.
Instead you are trampled on and cut,
You are lifeless and boring
And nobody cares about you.

Oliver Gunning (10)
Darite Primary School

Today I Saw . . .

Today I saw
The statued stones,
Jumbled, deserted trees.
Lifeless grass and mud,
Curling branches that haunt you.

Today I saw
The sun, so round and bright.
The calm, battered shed
And the everlasting smoke.

Today I saw
The lonely playground
That is no longer colourful and lively.
Fresh air, so cold and breezy
And the stone walls, grey and boring.

Beth Ridley (10)
Darite Primary School

Our School Grounds

Our school grounds has a wildlife part,
With a beautiful sun coming up.
In the school grounds, we have a shed,
An old, old shed with some flowers by the side of it.
We have a stony wall
Standing dead still on its own.
Trees waving in the soft wind, rough and bumpy.

Lauren Hedley (8)
Darite Primary School

Our School Grounds

Grey school ground's gutter.
Small, and is getting longer and longer.
Wet slimy, wet slimy and soggy.
Tall, dirty and dirty.

Courtney Sexton (7)
Darite Primary School

Our School Grounds

Tall rough branchy trees dangling in the wind.
A rusty brown slab placed on the ground, roaring when you step on it.
Grey long smooth gutter, standing still like a paper tube,
Green grass growing out of the ground, waving like a swing.
Brown gapped locked fence, opening like a squeaky mouse.
Prickly tangled brambles like a shoelace,
Red juicy berries like bouncy rubber balls,
A huge smooth wire.
The boiler, with a roar like a hungry lion, waiting to eat.

Gemma Wilkinson (7)
Darite Primary School

Our School Grounds

Fences enjoying the wind and dancing in the breeze,
And the cars go brum in the distance,
The houses go cold and wet,
The signs, yellow and black,
In a square.

Sammy Vine (8)
Darite Primary School

Our School Grounds

Tall grey trees dancing in the wind,
Green shimmering grass in the field.
Green crunchy moss hanging from the tree,
Green shimmering grass, swaying in the wind.
Crunchy leaves flying in the air like butterflies.

Chloe Gunning (8)
Darite Primary School

Our School Grounds

Green grass,
Blue sky,
Brown trees,
Transparent windows.
White houses,
Grey dustbins,
Red leaves.
Yellow leaves,
Green leaves,
Black dustbins.

Luca Martini (8)
Darite Primary School

Our School Grounds

Swishing trees in the breeze
And sharp rough rocks,
Green swaying grass,
Brown leafed tree,
Patterns in the old swaying tree,
Green leafed bushes.

Tristan Loughrey-Robinson (7)
Darite Primary School

Our School Grounds

Yellow sign
Coated with writing.
Humming of traffic
In the distance.
Chimneys smoking,
Smoke making
The shape of a snake.
Wind whistling
Through my ears.
White clear sky -
Not a cloud in sight.
The sound of
Water running
Through the
Drainpipes.
Brown wet
Fenceboards
Ready to
Get soaked.
Black tarmac
Laid out with
Six grey pillars.

Alex Sawley (8)
Darite Primary School

Our School Grounds

Excellent green slushy grass swaying from side to side.
Old wooden gate . . . waiting for somebody to come past it.
Rich brown soil like little imps wearing brown suits.
Trees with no leaves, like loads of people in a line
Grass coming out of walls like little people
Poking out their noses.
Sloping hill, like green pillows in a lump.
I hope one day that this will be the same place
But I know it will still be the same place.

Leeza Hodge (8)
Darite Primary School

Our School Grounds

Black cold tarmac laid on the ground,
Stone pillars round on the top,
A yellow sign coated in writing.
White clear sky,
Not a cloud in sight.
A brown stiff wooden fence,
Standing in the wind.

The smell of smoke moving through the air,
Old rusty drain full of water.
Humming of the traffic,
Moving through my ears.

Colourful blinds hand-made by children.
Huge hungry buildings, ready to swallow you,
Orange and white cones, a bit big for an ice cream.
Lights glimmer in the distance.

Ben Ackland (8)
Darite Primary School

Our School Grounds

Noisy, roaring boiler,
Grey slate and gutter.
Tiny little gutters on the ground.
Black doors shutting things away in the distance.

Nathaniel Vine (9)
Darite Primary School

Our School Grounds

The blowing of the swinging trees dancing like a boogie man.
Weak old trees settling in like a pair of old men.
Green grass wobbling about like great thick fields, diving in the sea.
Wind that's leaning like old men.
Trees standing still like secret spies.
Prickly leaves on the tree like a monster.
Fields overlapping each other, like breath.
Trees standing still, ready to approach space.
Grey twigs, like swords.

Luke Payne (9)
Darite Primary School

Our School Ground

Old rusty shed standing in the trees
doing nothing but listening to the breeze.
Quiet trees, grass and leaves,
joining in with the breeze.

Aaron Sexton (8)
Darite Primary School

Our School Grounds

Spiderwebs sucking in all the flies,
Green leaves covering the wall.
Tall thick walls all around,
Thin grey bars guarding the stairs.

Luke Serpell (9)
Darite Primary School

Our School Grounds

A slimy slug slithers along like a snake.
Shiny yellow light in the distance.
Spider webs like woolly jumpers.
Bright blue sky like the sea is in the sky,
Up high.
Dull black door like a man
In a black costume.

Barrie-Jon Hutton (8)
Darite Primary School

Our School Grounds

Tall bare trees standing
Still like packs of houses
In a row.

Plain white wall lying
Like a flat bit of
Paper on its own.

Shaped stones like
Round red rubber balls
All packed away.

Twiggy sticks sharp and
Stubby like a discarded pencil
A child once used.

Long spiral strips of ivy
Slithering round like
A long snake.

Dusty old playground
Played on by young
And old children.

Maybe one day we might
Paint the wall a rainbow
Or put flowerbeds around the wall -
This might happen.

Rebecca Ferguson (9)
Darite Primary School

Our School Grounds

Our school grounds has a wildlife part,
With a blue clear sky
And rocky old wall.
We have tall, brown, bare trees,
Swaying, dancing as they please.
Dead brown thorns,
Once so tall, but now like mice.
Whispering wind creeping through,
No wonder it's so cold and breezy.
The crooked old fences, rusty and rickety,
One day it will fall to pieces.
Everything. Quiet trees, grass and leaves,
No wonder it's a wildlife part.

Tilly Dimond (9)
Darite Primary School

The Sun

A white-hot pearl gleaming in space,
Feel its gentle rays warming your face.
A ball of fire sailing the white cloud,
Hovering there, so happy and proud.
Its warmth creeping everywhere,
Rippling a lion's brown shaggy hair.
This symbol of life shines bright,
In the sea there are crystals of light.
The sun warms the hearts of creatures alike.
From the birds up high to the pike.
The sun is our best friend,
It'll be there at the very end.

Rae Langton (11)
Grampound-With-Creed CE School

The Chip

Chips are fat
Chips are thin
Chips are round
Chips are flat
Chips you can dip in
Sauce like
Mayo, Ketchup,
Salad cream and
mushy peas.
Chips are yum!

Lucy Pearce (8)
Grampound-With-Creed CE School

Hatred

Hatred is a dark, despicable black colour
It tastes like a cold, dry Brussels sprout.
It smells as nasty as a dirty toilet.

It looks like a gone-off vulgar piece of cheese,
It sounds as ear-piercing as a scream
It feels like a forgotten soul.

Declan Byrne (10)
Grampound-With-Creed CE School

Dog

There once was a dog
Who sat on a frog
The frog was green
It had a sewing machine
Then the dog bounced
And the frog pounced
The frog made a bookmark
And then went to the park
It started to rain
It was a pain.

Sophie Bourne (8)
Grampound-With-Creed CE School

My Cat

There once was a cat
Who was ever so fat
He spent all his time
Singing a rhyme
And slept on a black furry mat.

Niamh Byrne (7)
Grampound-With-Creed CE School

The Royal Cat Of Cornwall

The royal cat of Cornwall
always has a hairball
giggles and jokes
kills half the folks
never dies
of course is wise.
Loves fish
on a dish
loves chasing a mouse
in his house.
Oh the royal cat of Cornwall.

Ciara Langton (7)
Grampound-With-Creed CE School

The Forest

Small red flowers bloom
The big forest brightens up and
Fills the dark, damp trees.

The white lilies grow
The sun shines on the forest
On a summer's day.

Dan Ford (10)
Grampound-With-Creed CE School

The Dodo

There was a bold Dodo
Whose name was Frodo
He was extremely smelly
And liked to live in a welly.
He had a girlfriend called Pogo.

Kester Westbrook Netherton (8)
Grampound-With-Creed CE School

A Naughty Dog

There was a dog
He collected a log
He was small and pink
He liked to stink
He liked chasing the frogs.

Ben Howe (7)
Grampound-With-Creed CE School

The Fat Parrot From York

There was a fat parrot from York
Who decided to perch on a fork
He suddenly slipped
And was shocked he flipped
With a horrible gurgling squawk.

Jack Nelson (10)
Grampound-With-Creed CE School

The Goat

There once was a grumpy old goat
Who had a very sore throat
He lived in a castle
Without any hassle
He had to go home over a moat.

Anna Venning (8)
Grampound-With-Creed CE School

Sunset

A crimson ruby
Resting on the horizon
Gazing at dolphins diving
And seals splashing
Starfish placed on their rocks
Amber rays reach out
To touch the golden colour-washed clouds
And from the east the darkness
Tiptoes in for the night.

Jasmine Tse (10)
Grampound-With-Creed CE School

The Moon

Gleaming in outer space,
Our hearts beating at a steady pace,
The sunlight beaming down to Earth,
Giving the light of the moon birth.
Keeping us living every day,
It's the symbol of life that makes us want to play,
Seeing the rocks on the moon,
Looking like a curved spoon,
You see it there every night,
Sitting there, so happy and bright.

Charlotte Juleff (11)
Grampound-With-Creed CE School

The Flying Pan

There was a weird man
He was flying in a pan
He said, 'You want a go?'
We said, 'No! No! No!'
And flew away, dancing the cancan.

Edward Tse (9)
Grampound-With-Creed CE School

Love

Love is red,
Love shines like a gleaming ruby
It tastes like a just picked strawberry.
It smells like a lawn that has just been cut
It sounds like a gentle breeze,
It feels like puppies' fur

Lucinda Thayers (7)
Grampound-With-Creed CE School

There Was A Fish

There once was a fish
Who ate his dish
He wanted to go for a walk
He saw his mate and had some pork
And that fish, had one wish.

Shane Williams (10)
Grampound-With-Creed CE School

The Lonely Train Boy

There he sits the train boy
Without his mum, without a toy.
He's in his little blanket,
He sings a song about his dad.
'I'm sad, I miss my dad.'
A man got money out of his pocket,
A lady got some out of her locket.
He's pale white, he sees a light
As a tear runs down his cheek
And round the corner, he had a little peek.
'Oh Dad, oh Dad, I am so sad.'
And I never saw the train boy again.

Sasha Fann (8)
Grampound-With-Creed CE School

Mr Feature

There was once a man called Mr Feature,
Who liked to turn into a creature.
He had a pet cat,
Who was very, very fat.
All the cat did was sleep,
And sometimes she would peep.
Mr Feature got her some food,
But like normal, she would be rude.
They got back in their car,
But went very, very, very far.

Lucas Swain (9)
Grampound-With-Creed CE School

Cakes

Cakes are tasty
Some are fat
Some have a lot of icing.
Cakes are really nice
To eat and some cakes
Have cherries on the top.

Eva Saul (8)
Grampound-With-Creed CE School

Cats

Cats like to play with bats
They sit on a smelly old mat
Cats jump high, right into the sky
And wear a black and white tie
They get in the mood
And eat too much food.

Jordan Still (8)
Grampound-With-Creed CE School

Plate Mouse

When I was eating my tea one day
My plate ran away!
I chased it around the house
Then it turned into a mouse.

Keziah Davies (9)
Grampound-With-Creed CE School

Today

Today I feel the wind touching my chest
So cold, the trees are as bare as a plain sheet of paper
I can smell the frilly green grass
I can hear the branches snapping and cracking

Today I feel the sun shining on my face
Footsteps stepping amongst the grass
I heard a plane gliding along the sky
I saw smoke twirling out of a little house

Today I heard the birds singing in the trees
I looked at the leaves on the ground
I heard a kitten crying for its mum
I saw an old man playing peek-a-boo behind a hill

Today I heard a woodpecker pecking at a tree
I heard stones hitting against the ground
I heard water falling into a drain
I heard feet swirling in the mud.

Aidan Whale (9)
Launceston CP School

Today

Today I can feel frozen leaves beneath my feet,
The birds singing like a choir,
I feel that whenever I move my feet, I hear crunching.

Today I smell smoke approaching from factories,
The dripping grass as wet as the ocean,
A gazebo that is as cold as an ice cube.

Today I can feel coldness on my face,
A cat which has fur as soft as a feather.
I can hear the water from the leisure centre.

Today I can feel crispy leaves on the steps as I walk up,
The pond frozen as ice.
Today the sun is just setting, but I can still feel the coldness.

Abigail Cleave (9)
Launceston CP School

Today

Today I heard
Bare trees shaking in the wind,
Leaves crunching under my feet,
Buzzing bees and singing birds,
Jets soaring through the sky,
A car's engine starting up,
A dog barking at its owner.

Today I saw
Moors glistening in the sun,
A blackbird gliding above my head,
Cat's eyes spying from a house,
Shadows in a pond waving about.

Today I smelt
Ivy letting off perfume,
Berries on a tree,
Oil running along the ground,
Leaves going rotten.

Today I felt
As cold as a flake of snow,
Puffs of wind whizz past my face.

William De Ferrars (9)
Launceston CP School

Why?

Why do I have to work?
Why do I have to walk miles each day?
Why do I get whipped like an out of control horse?

Why do I weep so much?
Why do I yell when my master beats me?
Why do I smell like a dustbin?

Why do I think that I want to die?
Why am I scared silly?
Why am I poor?

Why do I have rags on my back?
Why do I have no shoes?
Why do I have no money?

Why am I cold and dirty?
Why do I always get diseases?
Why do I feel dumb?

Why do I get whipped like I'm a piece of dirt?
Why do I feel weak?
Why do I die?

Cathryn Cruickshank (10)
Launceston CP School

Today

Today I felt . . .
The heat getting to my eyes as the sun drifted away into the distance.
The chilly wind getting to my face like a snowball.

Today I heard . . .
A roaring car flying past like a missile in the cold air.
A jet going as fast as the speed of light.

Today I saw . . .
The moors' gloominess in the distance and
The trees as tall as skyscrapers.

Today I smelt . . .
The sweat going to my head like a ball of fire.
A smell of smoke from the factory's chimney.

Bradley Cameron (9)
Launceston CP School

Today

Today I can hear a dog shouting for food.
Today I heard a bird singing a song.
Today my breath was as cold as the Arctic Sea.

I saw crispy green grass,
A car whizzing past.
Today I saw the sun shining like a diamond.
Today I saw the crystal clear sky.

Today I saw drifting, fluffy clouds.
Today I saw flowers as bright as a rainbow.
Today I saw leaves as slippery as ice.

Today I saw a jet zooming up into the sky.
Today I saw a magpie flying through the clouds.

Tyler Brooker (9)
Launceston CP School

Victorian Chimney Sweep

When I wake up I feel as weak as a twig,
My stomach is empty, like a dried up river.
I am as thin as a piece of paper.
I have to run as fast as I can to work.

My master thumps me like I am worthless,
My anger is rising. I want to hit him, but I know I can't.
Why do I have to go up the deadly chimney?
I've gone up the chimney.

I am already bleeding a bloodbath,
I can feel the blazing fire beneath me,
The soot blinding me,
My hands stinging, like I have been stung by a bee.

I am bruised and bleeding from the deadly chimney,
My legs are weak like a branch about to break.
I run home as fast as a cheetah.
I'm dreading tomorrow.

Adam Matthews (10)
Launceston CP School

Today

Today I feel as cold as the Arctic.
I can hear dogs barking as loud as thunder,
I can see a cat as quick as a cheetah,
And two adorable dogs walking slowly.

Today I can see a dead plant, as dead as a zombie.
I can hear the squirrel travelling in the trees.
I stood on the wet leaves and hard them crunch.
I heard people talking as loudly as a giant's footstep.

Today I can see the rooftops of the houses,
Grass as green as a Christmas tree.
I could see the bird's nest as deserted as an old graveyard.

The hut as empty as a lonely person,
I can see smoke drifting out of a chimney,
The stones clanking together by the pond.
I can see the berries growing in the bush.

Chantelle Oldaker (9)
Launceston CP School

Today I . . .

Today I saw . . .
People shivering in the crispy air,
My feet stamping on the crusty grass,
Birds shooting through the sky like bullets,
The sun shining like a golden sword.

Today I heard . . .
The trees cracking in the wind,
Birds diving for their meals,
My breath steaming like a train,
My heart beating like a boxer boxing a bag.

Today I felt . . .
The cold wind punching me in the chest,
The damp grass soaking my shoes.
I felt the chilly air freezing my numb fingers.
I felt my eyes watering from the bitter air.

Joshua McCabe (10)
Launceston CP School

Victorian Chimney Sweep

When I am walking I hear people laugh at me,
The wind howling like a dog,
My master standing staring, like his spirit is gone.
When he opens the door it creaks like a floorboard,
He pushes me like he iss going to kill me.
I climb like a bird flying with a broken wing,
My knee's wrecked, like breaking a plank of wood.
I can't see, the thick soot is blocking where I am going.
When I have finished, I hear the people laugh at me.

Tom Ellacott (10)
Launceston CP School

Today

Today I can hear the shiny leaves under my feet.
My head is spinning round and round.
I can see the clouds moulding into shapes.

The sun is only just peeking out,
Like a torch lighting the world,
The breeze flashing in my face,
Blowing my hair up, up, up above.

The hard wind blows strongly,
Making the trees look like shapes swirling round and round.
I feel frightened, for the trees look like faces.
The trees are waving side to side,
Crunching and calling in the wind,
Like they're trying to move.

Bethany Addicott (9)
Launceston CP School

Seagull

Seagull, seagull, carry me away,
Carry me away past the banana tree
So I can see the bobbing boats,
Red, green and blue,
Swinging side to side.

Seagull, seagull, carry me away,
Carry me away past the bobbing boats
So I can see the fish in the waters below,
Orange, yellow and rainbow-coloured,
Bobbing around.

Seagull, seagull, carry me away,
Carry me away past the fish below,
Back to where we started.

William Vanstone (10)
Launceston CP School

Today

Today I see leaves falling from the oak tree.
Today I see rainbow cars that sparkle in the sunlight.
Today I see gliding planes and wonder how they fly.
Today I see beautiful light that is as bright as the sunlight.
Today I see squirrels climbing their trees.
Today I see trees as tall as skyscrapers.
Today I see butterflies as beautiful as a flock of birds lifting off.
Today I see dog bins as smelly as a garbage truck.
Today I see pathways as thin as a stick.

Richard Burdon (10)
Launceston CP School

Today

Today I see wet stones near a shivering pond,
With rustling leaves nearby.
I am walking on wet grass,
My feet are freezing like ice.

Today I hear birds chirping away,
The monotonous bark of a furious dog,
People mumbling away with their friends,
A tick-tock of a watch.

Today I feel chilly,
The wind biting on my face,
Fresh grass touching my feet,
Trees surrounding the world.

Today I smell fresh-cut grass,
A squirrel running across the branches,
The smell of the swimming pool.
I hear children's pencils writing.

Hannah Perkins (9)
Launceston CP School

Today

Today I heard the roar of an engine,
Singing of birds,
Dogs barking loudly,
People standing on crunchy leaves.

Today I could see people walking dogs,
Smoke from factories,
Cars rushing past,
Planes resting in the air.

Today I felt the air blowing on my face,
Cold rushing in the breeze,
Lonely leaves blowing on the ground,
Drips of cold rain.

Today I saw a squirrel climbing for food,
A cloud glowing,
Flowers as cold as ice.

Abigael Stevenson (10)
Launceston CP School

It Was So Quiet I Heard . . .

It was so quiet I heard a pig painting.
It was so quiet I heard the sky skipping.
It was so quiet I heard the chimneys chattering.
It was so quiet I heard the clouds clapping.
It was so quiet I heard a baby bouncing.
It was so quiet I heard a boat bobbing.
It was so quiet I heard a starfish stretching.
It was so quiet I heard a crab crawling.
It was so quiet I heard a duck dancing.
It was so quiet I heard a pizza pop.
It was so quiet I heard a bug burp!

Joy Gibbs (7)
Launceston CP School

Give Yourself A Hug

(Based on 'Give Yourself a Hug' by Grace Nichols)

Give yourself a hug when you're feeling sad,
Give yourself a hug when you are feeling down,
Give yourself a hug when you've hurt yourself,
Give yourself a hug, a big, big hug,
And keep on singing,
'Only one in a million like me,
Only one in a million-billion-trillion-zillion like me!'

Kimberly Thomas (8)
Launceston CP School

Don't Call A Monkey Chubby Cheeks Before You Cross The Vines
(Based on 'Don't Call Alligator Long-Mouth Till You Cross The River' by John Agard)

Call Monkey chubby cheeks,
Call Monkey freckle face,
Call Monkey stumpy ears,
Call Monkey gigantic eyes,
Call Monkey narrow nostrils,
Call Monkey melting gum,
Call Monkey all dem rude words,
But better wait . . .
Till you cross the vines!

Megan Vanstone (7)
Launceston CP School

Call Elephant
(Based on 'Don't Call Alligator Long-Mouth Till You Cross The River' by John Agard)

Call Elephant grey face,
Call Elephant stinky breath,
Call Elephant fatty,
Call Elephant big body,
Call Elephant fat head,
Call Elephant tree wrecker,
Call Elephant all dem rude words,
But better wait till you cross the river!

Tristan Parsons (7)
Launceston CP School

Give Yourself A Hug
(Based on 'Give Yourself a Hug' by Grace Nichols)

Give yourself a hug when you are left out,
Give yourself a hug when you are poorly,
Give yourself a hug when you have been bad and you feel sad,
Give yourself a big enormous hug,
And keep on singing.

Jack Hogan (8)
Launceston CP School

Call Whale Fatty
(Based on 'Don't Call Alligator Long-Mouth Till You Cross The River' by John Agard)

Call Whale fatty,
Call Whale lumpy tail,
Call Whale dull skin,
Call Whale big mouth,
Call Whale long teeth,
Call Whale fat potato,
Call Whale all dem rude words,
But better wait 'til you cross the sea.

James Cleave (7)
Launceston CP School

Give Yourself A Hug
(Based on 'Give Yourself a Hug' by Grace Nichols)

Give yourself a hug when you're feeling like a slug,
Give yourself a hug when you're as small as a bug and feeling sad,
Give yourself a hug when you're feeling down and feeling ill,
Give yourself a hug when you deserve one,
Give yourself a hug, be proud of yourself,
And say, 'Only one in a million like me,
Only one in a milion-billion-trillion-zillion like me!'

Sebastian Fletcher (8)
Launceston CP School

Call Natalie's Rat . . .
(Based on 'Don't Call Alligator Long-Mouth Till You Cross The River' by John Agard)

Call Natalie's rat long tail,
Call Natalie's rat worm tail,
Call Natalie's rat skinny tail,
Call Natalie's rat baldy tail,
Call Natalie's rat string tail,
Call Natalie's rat all dem rude words
But better wait 'til you cross the carpet.

Josie Stevenson (7)
Launceston CP School

Call Snake
(Based on 'Don't Call Alligator Long-Mouth Till You Cross The River' by John Agard)
Call Snake bumpy tongue,
Call Snake fire breath,
Call Snake smelly,
Call snake smelly tail,
Call snake all dem rude words
But better wait 'til you cross the river!

Anne Mallett (8)
Launceston CP School

Give Yourself A Hug
(Based on 'Give Yourself a Hug' by Grace Nichols)

Give yourself a hug when you feel unloved,
Give yourself a hug when you feel a bit down,
Give yourself a hug when you're feeling sick,
Give yourself a hug when you're feeling cold,
Give yourself a hug when you're feeling tired,
And have a big yawn when you're cosy in bed,
Give yourself a hug - a big, big hug!
Give yourself a great big hug when you're very, very proud of yourself.

Naomi Choak (8)
Launceston CP School

Give Yourself A Hug
(Based on 'Give Yourself a Hug' by Grace Nichols)

Give yourself a hug when you feel like a bug,
Give yourself a hug when you don't feel snug,
Give yourself a hug when you feel like going down a plug
And keep on singing,
'Only one in a million like me,
Only one in a million-billion-trillion-zillion like me!'

Henry Williams (8)
Launceston CP School

Call Hippo Fat Belly
(Based on 'Don't Call Alligator Long-Mouth Till You Cross The River' by John Agard)

Call Hippo fat belly,
Call Hippo big mouth,
Call Hippo short tail,
Call Hippo long legs,
Call Hippo fatty,
Call Hippo dumb,
Call Hippo all dem rude words
But better wait till you cross the river!

Marcus Hill (8)
Launceston CP School

Gran, Can You Rap?

She rapped down town,
She rapped to the school,
She kept on rapping into the pool.
She rapped through the house,
She rapped upstairs,
She kept on rapping
And got eaten by bears!
And in the bear's tummy, this is what she said,
'I'm the best rapping gran this world's ever seen,
I'm a flip-flap, scritch-scratch, rap-rap queen!'

Thomas Gist (8)
Launceston CP School

Don't Call Giraffes Rude Names 'Til You Cross The Grass
(Based on 'Don't Call Alligator Long-Mouth Till You Cross The River' by John Agard)

Call giraffes rude names like long neck,
Call giraffes rude names like fat bum,
Call giraffes rude names like fatty,
Call giraffes all dem rude words
But better wait 'til you cross the grass.

Rebecca Vidler (7)
Launceston CP School

Gran, Can You Rap?
(Based on 'Gran Can You Rap' by Jack Ousbey)

She rapped through the house, past me and my brother,
She rapped quickly past even my mother,
She's the best rapping gran this world's ever seen,
She's a flip-flop, slip-slap, rap-rap queen.

Kayleigh Jenkins (8)
Launceston CP School

Don't Call A Millipede Long Legs
(Based on 'Don't Call Alligator Long-Mouth Till You Cross The River' by John Agard)

Call Millipede lots of legs,
Call Millipede small head,
Call Millipede milli-lump,
Call Millipede no head,
Call Millipede trip over legs,
Call Millipede long body,
Call Millipede all dem rude words
But better wait 'til you cross your garden.

Lewis Matthews (8)
Launceston CP School

Don't Call A Jaguar Jet Legs
(Based on 'Don't Call Alligator Long-Mouth Till You Cross The River' by John Agard)

Call Jaguar jet legs,
Call Jaguar jealous jigsaw,
Call Jaguar all dem rude words
But better wait 'till you cross the jungle.

Sophie Danson (7)
Launceston CP School

Love

Love is red like roses,
It feels like love,
It tastes like chocolate,
It sounds like your heart,
It looks like kissing,
It smells like bluebells.

Jordan Karkeek (7)
Launceston CP School

Love

Love is red like roses,
It looks like hugging and kissing,
It smells like sweet peas,
It feels like butterflies,
It reminds me of daisies.

Jessica Platt (7)
Launceston CP School

Sadness

Sadness is black like the night sky,
It looks like a ripped teddy,
It tastes like burnt toast,
It smells like a dead pony,
It feels like someone punching you.

Cameron Hollidge (7)
Launceston CP School

Happiness

Happiness is gold like a golden deer,
It reminds me of Christmas,
It feels like snowballs crashing against the wall,
It tastes like Bonfire Night,
It looks like a cute polar bear,
It smells like a roast dinner,
It sounds like Santa's sleigh bells.

Lucy Cameron (7)
Launceston CP School

Listen

Listen to the angels playing the harp,
The birds singing beautiful songs,
The rustling of trees.
Listen to the wind puffing away the leaves,
The witches' laughs crying in the wind,
The raindrops dropping on the ground,
The woodpecker asleep in its nest,
A new baby bird crying softly
And a wild pig taking a bath.

Natalie Stevenson (8)
Launceston CP School

It's So Quiet

It's so quiet I can hear the yellow sun rising,
The fluffy clouds moving
And a tiny ant breathing.

It's so peaceful I can hear a large cat moving,
The huge world moving
And the light of dawn breaking.

It's so silent I can hear the smallest fish moving,
A bright light turning on and off
And a calm dove flying.

Robyn Land (9)
Launceston CP School

Clouds

In the clouds I see . . .
My nan drinking a pint,
A dog getting chased by a woolly mouse,
A stranger talking to a lady,
And my cute cuddly cat going to sleep.

In the clouds I see . . .
A clown sitting on his bed made out of pies,
Henry VIII, the six wives and the children,
And my grandpa and old cat who are dead.

In the clouds I see . . .
My family in a lovely photo,
My mum buying me a pony,
Elli, Mrs Rutherford's dog,
And my friends making me a party.

Bethany Chapman (8)
Launceston CP School

Listen

This morning I saw clouds,
They made me think about silence.
Listen to trees blowing and
Rumbling and grumbling.
I can hear my heart beating.
The clouds are swaying.
Think about feelings.

I can hear myself breathing,
Oh so silent and peaceful,
I could hear children in schools playing.

Listen to rubbish rustling,
Listen to babies crying,
Listen to sea gushing.

Abby Bounsall (9)
Launceston CP School

In My Magic Box

In my magic box I have
A 101-year-old cat
That can do anything,
A mouse that talks
French, English, Latin, Spanish,
A toy train that is 1,000kg,
That goes 1,009 miles per hour,
A tiny dinosaur that can
Run faster than the speed of light.

In my magic box I have a sweet
That can turn you into
Anything you want,
A dog that miaows
And looks like a cat,
A book that can take you
Where you want to go,
A box that makes you into a
World class football player.

Alexander Shopland (8)
Launceston CP School

Clouds

In the clouds I see
My dead grandad and
My two ancient cats,
I imagine my great-grandparents,
I see a lady chatting up my dad,
Auntie and Uncle bringing their dog Brillo down,
I see my brother sitting on a chair
And I imagine when my mum was young.

In the clouds I see
A furious dragon breathing hot fire,
Some letters that say, 'Come and play'.
I see the wall hanging that I'm sewing
And I imagine voices saying things to me.

Claire Downing (9)
Launceston CP School

Listen

Listen to the angels singing songs gracefully,
The butterflies collecting pollen,
Birds building delicate nests,
Caterpillars chomping leaves.
Listen to the bumblebees buzzing away,
A horse trotting down the lane noiselessly,
Leaves rustling silently.

Laura Champ (8)
Launceston CP School

Listen

Listen, hear the footsteps of people far, far away,
The smashing of a river,
The rustling of leaves on a sunny day.
Listen, hear the people talking of a far distant land,
The sound of water, the trickling of the sea,
The stamping of a rhino,
The banging of people knocking on other people's doors,
The snapping of branches breaking off trees.

Liam Sloan (8)
Launceston CP School

Clouds

In the clouds I can see . . .
An angel staring back at me,
A teenager arguing with her parents,
A dragon breathing bright red fire
Into a windowpane.

I can see in the clouds . . .
A unicorn riding through an oasis in a desert,
A clown throwing custard pies at all the guests,
A sun setting around the misty moon.

I can see in the clouds . . .
Caterpillars munching a juicy leaf,
Giraffes walking through the safari,
Tarzan swinging through the African jungle.

In the clouds I can see . . .
Monsters having a massive food fight,
Dolphins diving into the deep blue sea,
Water running through a dirty stream.

Casey Nolan (9)
Launceston CP School

In The Clouds I saw . . .

In the clouds I saw . . .
A lion's mane as yellow as a sunflower,
A giraffe's neck as tall as a skyscraper,
A fluffy white bed as soft as blankets,
A key from a long lost treasure chest.

In the clouds I saw . . .
A drunken young man with a beard,
A crab with claws as sharp as granite,
A shoe that looks like a pebble,
A pansy as bright as the sun.

In the clouds I saw . . .
The face of a newborn baby,
A cat as silent as a mouse,
A tiger as fierce as a leopard in a bad mood,
A sheet as huge as a double bed.

Charlotte Duff (8)
Launceston CP School

Horses

The horse's mane sways like a busy tree,
The tail is long and silky.
Eyes like sparkling jewels.
The neigh is a thunder.
She gallops like the wind rushing by.

Megan Jackson (8)
Launceston CP School

Listen

Listen to the clouds blushing
Against the houses.
Listen to feet clapping
On the ground.
Listen to the thunder
Crashing on the rocks.
Listen to the river
Flowing carefully.
Listen to the fish's tail
Wiggling in the river.

Sophie Cameron (8)
Launceston CP School

In My Magic Box
(Based on ' Magic Box' by Kit Wright)

In my magic box . . .
I'll have in there the smell of a biro pen,
The smell of the fresh air,
The smell of fresh orange juice,
The smell of the fire.

In my magic box . . .
I'll have the skin of a sausage,
The skin of a snake,
The skin of a caterpillar,
The skin of a tiger.

In my magic box . . .
I'll have in there the picture of a forest,
The picture of a town,
The picture of a football stadium,
The picture of a classroom.

Joshua Harris (9)
Launceston CP School

In My Box
(Based on 'Magic Box' by Kit Wright)

In my box I have the tip of a dragon's tongue.
A sip of some fine wine.
The blood of my uncle Richard.
A piece of a sailing ship.
A medal from the world war.

My box is lined with pure gold.
The lid is dotted with glittering diamonds.
My box has a lock
Which only I can see.

Elias O'Neill (8)
Launceston CP School

Magic Box
(Based on 'Magic Box' by Kit Wright)

I will put in my box a tiger's first word,
A vicious frog with a football top on him.

I will put in my box a magic machine,
A Ferrari 500 with a sticker on it,
And an evil elf.

I will put in my box a lazy cow,
A cool motorbike with a turbo
And a shrinking car.

I will put in my box a talking telephone
And a red arrow.

It has 10 stars on the lid.
Its hinges are made of sharks' teeth.

George Habgood (8)
Launceston CP School

Listen

Listen to the sound of waves in the sea
Crashing against the rocks,
And the seagulls crying aloud.
Listen to the clouds moving
And the clock ticking.
Listen to the tap dripping, the cows mooing
And the butterflies' wings in the wind.
The sound of my favourite band
Playing in the distance.
Listen to the rustling of the leaves,
The rainbow appearing from the rain,
And the chameleon's tongue
Flying back and forward.
Listen to the keys on the keyboard being tapped,
And the radio playing faintly.

Thomas Clogg (9)
Launceston CP School

Clouds

In the clouds I can see a fearless dragon,
Breathing out fiery breath,
A selfish bear greedily eating heaps of yellow honey,
And a beautiful young lady
Dancing with an ugly old man.

In the clouds I noticed
A gorgeous angel,
Beautifully singing around an ugly oak tree,
A rich queen with a spotty toad in her hands
And a massive elephant,
Happily blowing water over an angry zookeeper.

In the clouds I saw a sporty giraffe
Excitedly playing a fun game of badminton,
A bossy snake cooking delicious chocolate chip cookies
And a bold horse fearlessly fighting a strong knight.

In the clouds I watched a rotten skeleton
Playing cards,
A bouncy kangaroo chasing a petrified little duckling
And a tired teenager idling
On a wobbly jelly sofa.

Keziah Parnell (9)
Launceston CP School

Animals

An alligator ate an anxious ant.
Captain Casey caught a crazy camel.
Dangerous Daniel dreamed about dragons.
Frosty frogs froze on Friday.
Tall Toby tickled two tiny tigers.
An Easter eagle echoed easily.
A lively lizard limped lamely.
An eager eel electrocuted an enormous eagle.

Tobias Knights (8)
Launceston CP School

My Magic Box
(Based on 'Magic Box' by Kit Wright)

In my magic box I will put . . .
the smell of fresh air,
then the aeroplanes that are rushing about,
I will put in some of the fastest racing cars ever.
In my magic box I will put . . .
some of the real ancient dinosaurs.
My magic box will have in it
every country in the world.
In my magic box I will put . . .
one of the longest caves in the universe.
I'll have in there the moon and stars.
I will have in it an enormous rock.
In my magic box I'll have everything,
Then in my magic box I will put . . .
the magic of my imagination.

Thomas Davison (9)
Launceston CP School

Magic Box
(Based on 'Magic Box' by Kit Wright)

In my magic box I will put my hope.
I will put secrets in it.
I will keep my trust in it.
I will put a statue of God.
My magic box looks like a chest with shells around the edge.
My magic box has gold pebbles in the middle.

Daniel Bradshaw (9)
Launceston CP School

Magic Box
Based on 'Magic Box' by Kit Wright)

In my magic box I will put . . .
A baby's first smile,
A snowman,
A fairy with a bee hat, or a magic star
And the song of a bird.
In my magic box I will put . . .
A dozen jewels.
The whitest snow on Earth,
Melted lava from Thailand
And the swiftest guard dogs with iron teeth.
In my magic box I will put . . .
A golden, bright trophy.
The brightest star and moon,
Silver and gold bells
And cockle shells.
My magic box is made of . . .
Red dragon's toes for hinges.
The lock is made of lion's teeth
And decorated with two diamonds
Shaped like a star.
Inside is lovely soft red leather.

Heather Davey (8)
Launceston CP School

Dog

Its nose is like a piece of charcoal.
Ears like radar.
Growl like a horn.
Fur like a piece of wool.
Legs like tree stumps.
It digs like a digger.
It runs like a racing car.
Its teeth are as sharp as daggers.
Eyes like binoculars.
Tail as long as a plant.
Paws as big as dinner plates.
Claws like swords.
It swims like a fish.

Aron Finnimore (9)
Launceston CP School

The Cheetah

Yellow as a banana
Black spots like a bucket of coal.
Fast as a rocket
Teeth like needles
Tail as long as a garden hose.
Claws as sharp as knives.
Roar as loud as motorbike.
Thin as a chip.

Faron Tilley (8)
Launceston CP School

I Want To Paint . . .

I want to paint a glistening starfish
gently bobbing through the seaweed.

I want to paint a multicoloured flower
that gives the smell of a hundred red roses.

I want to paint a mountain
with snow as soft as the clouds.

I want to paint a real life ladybird
with pink ballerina shoes and tiara.

Zara Choak (10)
Launceston CP School

There Was A Young Girl

There was a young girl called Sam
She ate loads of ham and then ran.
She took her dog Rover
Who tripped and fell over
Then they rolled right into a dam.

Mandy Sillifant (10)
Launceston CP School

Wind

I can blow things down,
I can spin things round and round.

I can make a great noise,
I can even have fun with the boys.

I can run and hide
Or I can swish and slide.

I can be good and bad,
I can be happy and sad.

Hannah Barnes (10)
Launceston CP School

December

De snow, de sleet, de lack of heat,
De wishy washy sunlight,
De lip turn blue, de cold 'achoo!'
De runny nose, de frostbite.

De eyes a glow, de skies of snow
De shall we have a snow fight?
De toasty feet, de fire's heat,
De star shine and de moon light.

De frost all around, de slidy ground
De Christmas tills a-ringin',
De seasonal sights, de twinkly lights
De Christmas songs for singing.

De lights are on, de day is done,
De pansies, dey all wither,
De cats dey sleep, de dogs dey weep,
Dey were left outside under de heather!

De day it comes, de kids dey slums,
Dey can't wait to see Santa,
De Christmas tree, a perfect beauty,
Dey don't find nothing but Fanta.

De mud, de grime, de slush, de slime,
De place gloomy since November,
De sinkin' heart is just the start o'
De wintertime -
December.

William Samuels (11)
Launceston CP School

Untitled

The woman who loved to eat liver,
Strolled up to the bridge all a quiver.
She gave a loud cough,
Her right leg fell off,
Blood gleamed as it floated down river.

Duncan Whale (11)
Launceston CP School

Who Am I?

Food eater
Mice chaser
Chair scratcher
Milk drinker
Day sleeper
Night stalker
Fur licker
Tree climber.

A catalogue
To make me a cat.

Alexandra Wilton (10)
Launceston CP School

What Am I?

Fast swimmer
Fish eater
Ocean dweller
High jumper
Squeal maker
People lover
Show performer
Song singer.

Robyn Wadman (10)
Launceston CP School

I Want To Paint . . .

I want to paint . . .
the boiling hot sun
with a slight breeze of fresh air.
I want to paint . . .
a lion holding hands with a zebra
and no hostility.
I want to paint . . .
a thousand rainforests
that will never be chopped down.
I want to paint . . .
animals that will never experience any cruelty.
I want to paint . . .

Harry Pooley (11)
Launceston CP School

Lightning

I can flash through the streets without any warning,
and last all night long and right through the morning.
I can run at the enormous speed of light,
or I can give you a quick, terrible fright.
I develop on the rough, raging seas,
or I can break down huge willow trees.
I can zip through any strong metal,
like a knife through a beautiful red petal.
I can give you all your great power,
or I can break down the Eiffel Tower.

Joshua Jackson (11)
Launceston CP School

There Was An Old Man . . .

There was an old man from Bodmin Moor
Who heard an awful tiger's roar
He cuddled his wife
Who had come from Fife
But they were both knocked down to the floor.

Lewis Holden (10)
Launceston CP School

Boattripaphobia

I am afraid of boat trips,
Like a worm is petrified of a bird,
Like a rugby pitch is scared of studs,
Like shampoo is terrified of a plughole,
Like a pencil is frightened of a sharpener,
Like paint is horrified of a paintbrush,
I am afraid of boat trips.

Lucy Perry (10)
Launceston CP School

Today

Today I saw the sun shining on my face.
Today I saw leaves falling off trees.
Today I saw dogs running.
Today I heard dogs barking louder than a church bell rings.
Today I felt the cold wind blowing.
Today I saw the cars driving fast.
Today I could smell the fresh air.
Today I saw trees swaying.
Today I saw three dogs playing happily.
Today I heard lorries reversing back.
Today I saw dogs wandering around.
Today I tasted salt and vinegar crisps.
Today I saw money on the table.
Today I heard cars driving outside.
Today I saw cows at the farm.
Today I heard music playing.
Today I heard doors closing.

Garod Gregory (9)
Launceston CP School

The Magic Box
(Based on 'Magic Box' by Kit Wright)

I'll put in my box . . .
The icing on a slab of cake,
The time of the Ice Age with mammoths so great
And an annoying gnome that's manageable to hate.
I'll put in my box . . .
An English fire that boils to the bone,
A galaxy of new plants and a new milky way
And a magnanimous supermarket where you don't have to pay.
I'll put in my box . . .
A capsizing ship with frenzied people,
A lens of a camera that's blue, black and red
And an old man who's going to bed.
I'll put in my box . . .
The sound of the ocean roaring
And on my box I will put a star of life that is tiny and cute
And a firework display in front of the sun's ray.
I'll finally put in my box . . .
The recipe of truth and an aerosol of water
And this is just the start of the objects you admire
Because there's loads more things in the world
To be amazed by and simply desire.

Steven Hooper (11)
Luxulyan Primary School

Happiness

Happiness is yellow like golden sand from popular beaches
and the really bright sun coming towards you.

Happiness is yellow like a golden goose's egg
and the sound of seagulls squealing.

Happiness feels like you're really, really enjoying yourself
and looks like a really, really bright yellow.

Happiness is yellow like the middle of a well cooked egg
that somebody's about to eat.

Simon Crocker (10)
Luxulyan Primary School

My Little Monster

A little monster
A trouble maker
A house breaker
A milk lover
A nose picker
A clothes wrecker
A vomit spitter
A money waster
A floor crawler
A food thrower
A hair puller
A nappy wetter
An attention seeker
A squealer
An expert on escaping
A perfect dribbler.

(A baby)

Luke Rowe
Luxulyan Primary School

A World On A Different Planet!

(Based on 'Magic Box' by Kit Wright)

In my box I will put . . .
A bird of prey, flapping fiercely like a ball of hot flames,
An unknown mystery never to be solved,
A twinkling star, from a long-lost land,
An injured petal trying to defeat gravity,
A tunnel which never ends,
A world without people, a very tranquil place,
A rose opening to the floating fresh air,
A desperate county without a sky,
A universe without any war,
A moon without a face,
A sun without a temperature,
A smile upon a young one's face.
I will put in my box . . .
A warm, soft feather floating steadily down
To the old, ancient, broken floor,
A crying wave being broken down by the roaring lion,
A simmering hot ice cube melting down very rapidly,
A glass of water from the Lake District,
A leaping cheetah as slow as a snail,
A joke from a lifeless witch,
A toe from a dying hyena.
I will play in the box . . .
Till the horse stops neighing
And the people stop praying.

Heather Charlesworth (11)
Luxulyan Primary School

My Magic Box
(Based on 'Magic Box' by Kit Wright)

In my magic box I'll put . . .
a ruby red elephant, worth millions of pounds,
Saturn's moons glistening brightly,
immortality encrusted in silver and gold.

I'll put in my box . . .
a fire made from water, that needs wood to put it out,
an invisibility shawl that is treasured very much,
a dead moon, lost forever.

My box will hold . . .
a jet-black feather gracefully dancing in the air,
an immense sea-blue whale darting swiftly in the dazzling ocean,
used gravity that has lost its magical forces.

My box would be incomplete without . . .
stardust from years ago,
forgotten countries from under the sea,
one thousand pennies found on the same dusty lane.

My box is designed like a scarlet tiger
with sky-blue stripes, studded with emeralds.
I'll sit in my box and think about all the secrets in my life.

Nicola Smith (9)
Luxulyan Primary School

Magic Box
(Based on 'Magic Box' By Kit Wright)

I will put into my box . . .
The shine of a delicate star
Floating in the midnight sky.
The roar of a lion
Pouncing on its prey.
A minute spot from a precious ladybird
Scuttling across granite rocks.
The final whisper of an old man dying.
I will put into my box . . .
A spot of warm breath
Steaming up a stained glass window.
A chunk of green sky.
A buzz from a bumblebee
And a sting from a wasp.
A fluffy, silky, smooth feather
Gracefully tumbling through the warm summer's air.
I will put into my box . . .
A heart from a flea
Being scraped off a dog's fur.
The eyeball from a pig.
An author illustrating books.

I constructed my box of gold and silver
With moons on the top
And stars on the edge.
I'll climb Mount Everest
And live with my box forever.

Lauren Hoskin (10)
Luxulyan Primary School

My Magic Box
(Based on 'Magic Box' by Kit Wright)

I will put in my box . . .
a galloping horse in a field.
I will put in my box . . .
Mars floating around space.
I will put in my box . . .
a dragon exploding.
I will put in my box . . .
the sun bright as ever.

I will put in my box . . .
a star falling from space.
I will put in my box . . .
the peace of harmony.
I will put in my box . . .
a blue whale gliding
across the ocean.
I will put in my box . . .
air invisible as dust.

Benjamin Bond (9)
Luxulyan Primary School

Imaginary Box
(Based on 'Magic Box' by Kit Wright)

I'll put in my box . . .
A bear catching fish in a stream,
A horse galloping across the moor,
A cheetah scampering after its food.
I will put in my box . . .
The seven seas,
A bouquet of freshly scented flowers,
A tooth sharp as a knife,
A whisper of air going through me.
I will put in my box . . .
A dolphin skimming across the water,
The highest peak of a mountain,
A frost of a morning.
I will put in my box . . .
The sound of the night in Spain,
A mark of charcoal,
The salt of the sea.
I will put in my box . . .
Ink spreading on a paper,
A colossal whale gliding in the shimmering, crystal-clear ocean.
I will run in my box
Around the Olympic circuit.

William George (11)
Luxulyan Primary School

My Magic Box
(Based on 'Magic Box' by Kit Wright)

In my box I will put . . .
The first queen of England,
A huge gold elephant,
A red rose from the Garden of Eden,
The last smile of a dying old granny.

In my box I will put . . .
A fireball from a fire-breathing monster,
The red-hot stones from Mars,
A glass of water from the big, wide blue sea.

In my box I will put . . .
A pretty white feather dancing in the light breeze,
The stars and moon,
A pink cloud higher than the sun,
A golden leaf from an old oak tree.

In my box I will put . . .
Peace, harmony, love and fun,
The hinges of my box will be made out of a whale's tooth.
There will be secrets in my box in the corners where nobody can see.

Millie Jones (10)
Luxulyan Primary School

Magic Box
(Based on 'Magic Box' by Kit Wright)

I will put in my box . . .
The fear of a man going to war
The peace of a dead leaf
The breath of a dragon
The heartbeat of a soldier
The explosion of an old star
The footprints of a dinosaur
The gravity of the Earth
The cloud that hangs round the pond
The air
The fire of the sun
The heat of a bonfire
The cold, dirty water of a pond
The feelings of a raindrop
The glistening of a newborn star
The soft, dry feather of a blue tit swooping through the pale blue sky
The cold ice-biting air from the freezing South Pole.

I'll fly my box to the other side of the world
And see animals I've never seen before.

Jamie Jepson (11)
Luxulyan Primary School

Feelings

Anger is black like a book without pictures.
Anger is black like bubbling oil.
Anger feels like a jagged stone.
Anger sounds like crows squawking.
Anger is black like a very stiff suit.
Like a black, sticky pal and a very deep hole.

Josh Jepson (9)
Luxulyan Primary School

The Magic Box
(Based on 'Magic Box' by Kit Wright)

I will put in my box . . .
A snake slithering up a tree.
Four dragons breathing flames.
A school with children running to their homes.

I will put in my box . . .
A killer whale wailing in the big, big ocean
And the breeze blowing the clouds.

Eddie Crocker (8)
Luxulyan Primary School

Change

Seas deep
Crabs creep
Buildings high
People sigh
Forests cleared
People feared
Natural life
Starting to die

People fight
Day and night
From one to ten
They run from men
Mother Nature
With her might

Horses rear
Birds peer
Plants shrivel
People's knives
End lives
The world is changing
And you can't stop it.

Alex Nankivell (11)
Luxulyan Primary School

My Kennings

A mouth snapper
A meat eater
A deadly creature
A four-legged creature.

Ashley Hick (10)
Luxulyan Primary School

My Magic Box
(Based on 'Magic Box' by Kit Wright)

I will put in my box . . .
A rapid flowing through a river
A golden goose
A man on a flying boat.

I will put in my box . . .
An oompaloompa that can run a marathon
An elephant as light as a feather
A cat that can run as fast as a cheetah.

I will put in my box . . .
A brick the size of a car
A holiday as a workday
A workday as a holiday.

I will put in my box . . .
A puffin with a silver beak
An African sardine with no bones
A moon with no light.

I will put in my box . . .
An apple that looks like a human the size of a dog
A sun with no heat.

I will put in my box . . .
An extra planet
A final season
A caterpillar that's 30cm long
And that's what I will put in my box.

Eddie George (8)
Luxulyan Primary School

Happiness

Happiness is yellow like a flower.
Happiness feels like you're in a dream.
Happiness sounds like children playing.
Happiness feels like it's the best day of your life.
Happiness is like you're at a party.
Happiness is like you've won a race.

Eve Pettican (7)
Luxulyan Primary School

My Magic Box
(Based on 'Magic Box' by Kit Wright)

In my magic box . . .
I will put the soul of a unicorn
The Earth's middle core.

In my box . . .
Are three dinosaurs that survived the asteroid.

In my box I will put . . .
An ancient ancestor
And a Chinese dragon.

In my box . . .
There are all the seas, rivers and oceans
Three of the most mythical monsters in history
And every child's happiest dream.

In this particular box . . .
There are ten playground children
Seven violent sea monsters
Four Hindu warriors
And one of God's creations.

Samuel Hunt (8)
Luxulyan Primary School

The Playground

Best place of all
Children giggling
Naughty happening
Running feet
Pattering down
Shrieking shouts
Silence, stands
In the middle
No-man's-land
Standing lines
Hurry inside
To the warmth.

Where am I?
Playground.

Jennifer Wade (10)
St Day & Carharrack Community School, Burnwithan

The Playground

Children laughing
Teachers moaning
Screaming, shouting
Being silly
Loud children
Football flying
Juniors skipping
Telling tales
Happy children
Soft air
Ottilie screaming
Gate banging.

Where am I?
Answer: the playground.

Hannah Bown (9)
St Day & Carharrack Community School, Burnwithan

The Playground

Muddy puddles
Scuffed up grass
Footballs getting booted
Children sliding
Whistles screeching
People cheering
Ref blowing
Getting dirty
Children crying.

Where am I?
The playground.

Stephen Trenoweth (9)
St Day & Carharrack Community School, Burnwithan

The Playground

Children's laughter
Teacher natter
Juniors scoring
Hopscotch jumping
Dustbin clanging
Coats rustling
Door banging
People falling
Infants chasing
Getting moody
Moaning, groaning
Telling teachers.

Where am I?
The playground.

Tyler Truman (9)
St Day & Carharrack Community School, Burnwithan

The Playground

Screaming children
Moaning, groaning
Telling lies
Juniors moaning
Infants groaning
Adults shouting
Telling secrets
Munching, crunching
Children laughing
Hopscotch - jumping
Swishing coats
Swishing hair.

Where am I?
The playground.

Sarah Collett (10)
St Day & Carharrack Community School, Burnwithan

The Playground

Run, run, eat a bun
Happy children play with a toy gun
Children laughing, giggling, screaming
Teachers shouting, happy and laughing
Singing, dancing, happy and playful
Running round, happy and joyful
Going round in circles, having a good time
Magic's in the air as a butterfly goes by!
Playing, jumping, under the sky.

Where am I?
The playground.

Gillian Rapson (9)
St Day & Carharrack Community School, Burnwithan

A Classroom

Scribble, scribble
Working out
'I'm waiting'
'Stop and look'
'Keep thinking'
'Use your brain'
'Have a nice playtime'
'I'm stuck'
'What's the answer?'
'What does that say?'
'I can't do that'
'That's easy'

Where am I?
Answer: a classroom.

Samantha Dyer (9)
St Day & Carharrack Community School, Burnwithan

The Dinner Hall

Chatter, natter
Cutlery scraping
Food smelling
Tables banging
Staff shouting
Children munching
Food crunching
Munch, munch
Eating lunch.

Where am I?
The dinner hall.

Julia Braddon (9)
St Day & Carharrack Community School, Burnwithan

The School Playground

Children chatting
Adults nagging
Giggle, fiddle
Screaming, shouting
Enjoying playing
Wind waving
Bad, good
All we should
Playing, fighting
Totter potter
Big feet stamping
Chitter-chatter.

Where am I?
The school playground.

Logan Reynolds (10)
St Day & Carharrack Community School, Burnwithan

A Football Match

Feet patters
Rubbish splatters
Wrappers creasing
Children leaping
Adults shouting
No one doubting
Everyone screeching
Sometimes fighting
Let loose imagination
In the nation
Whistle blows
Everyone goes.

Where am I?
A football match.

Nessa Cawte (10)
St Day & Carharrack Community School, Burnwithan

Night-Time
(Based on 'Morning' by Grace Nichols)

Night-time comes
with the soft stars twinkling.

Night-time comes
with the warm bath steaming.

Night-time comes
with the hot fire gleaming.

Night-time comes
with the trees howling.

Night-time comes
with the cats all prowling.

Night-time comes
with my dad snoring.

Night-time comes
with the teapot pouring.

Night-time comes
with my warm bed waiting.

Ellie Sayer (10)
St Mary's CE Primary School, Truro

Night
(Based on 'Morning' by Grace Nichols)

Night comes
with stars twinkling.

Night comes
with the moonlight glistening.

Night comes
with owls whistling.

Night comes
with the fire crackling.

Night comes
with the hot bath bubbling.

Night comes
with the old trees moaning.

Night comes
with my dad snoring.

Night comes
with the wolves howling.

Night comes
to drag me into bed.

Felicity Hamilton (10)
St Mary's CE Primary School, Truro

Evening
(Based on 'Morning' by Grace Nichols)

Evening comes
with the sky darkening.

Evening comes
with the moonlight shining.

Evening comes
with stars glistening.

Evening comes
with owls hooting.

Evening comes
with the sound of sizzling.

Evening comes
with TVs talking.

Evening comes
with children sleeping.

Evening comes
with people snoring.

Evening comes
to put me into bed.

Harriet Skidmore (10)
St Mary's CE Primary School, Truro

Night-Time
(Based on 'Morning' by Grace Nichols)

Night comes
with the stars twinkling.

Night comes
with the moon sparkling.

Night comes
with sausages sizzling.

Night comes
with the kettle whistling.

Night comes
with vegetables roasting.

Night comes
with people eating.

Night comes
with people sleeping.

Night comes
with the door being bolted *shut!*

Cara Loukes (10)
St Mary's CE Primary School, Truro

Evening
(Based on 'Morning' by Grace Nichols)

Evening comes
'What's cooking?'

Evening comes
Sausages are sizzling.

Evening comes
The bath's running.

Evening comes
It's time for relaxing.

Evening comes
The stars are twinkling.

Evening comes
The moon is glowing.

Evening comes
The owls are hooting.

Evening comes
Everybody's sleeping.

Evening comes
It's time for bed.

Tristan Latarche (10)
St Mary's CE Primary School, Truro

Night Comes
(Based on 'Morning' by Grace Nichols)

Night comes
when the stars are twinkling.

Night comes
when the moon is sparkling.

Night comes
when some people are eating.

Night comes
when doors are opening.

Night comes
when people are sleeping.

Night comes
when people are snoring.

Night comes
when the fire is burning.

Night comes
when everyone is lying.

Night comes
to drag me into bed.
Boss - women - night.

Hannah Cavill (9)
St Mary's CE Primary School, Truro

Night
(Based on 'Morning' by Grace Nichols)

Night comes
with people sleeping.

Night comes
with stars twinkling.

Night comes
with clocks ticking.

Night comes
with robbers thieving.

Night comes
with a bath so relaxing.

Night comes
with children cuddling.

Night comes
with everyone snuggling.

Night comes
with bats flattering.

Before morning comes
boss - women - night.

Hannah Vaughan (10)
St Mary's CE Primary School, Truro

Night

(Based on 'Morning' by Grace Nichols)

Night comes
With birds screeching.

Night comes
With Dad snoring.

Night comes
With stars twinkling.

Night comes
With people dreaming.

Night comes
With lightning crashing.

Night comes
With trees swaying.

Night comes
With the windows banging.

Night comes
With woodland creatures peeping.

Night comes
With all who are gazing.

Night comes to drag me into bed
Boss-man - night.

Luke Dehaan (9)
St Mary's CE Primary School, Truro

Night
(Based on 'Morning' by Grace Nichols)

Night comes
When all are sleeping,

Night comes
When all are weeping,

Night comes
When all are boring,

Night comes
When owls are hooting.

Night comes
When all are snoring.

Night comes
When cars are tooting.

Night comes
When wolves are howling,

Night comes
When all are scowling.

Night comes to drag
Me into bed.

Rhiannon Boon (9)
St Mary's CE Primary School, Truro

Night-Time
(Based on 'Morning' by Grace Nichols)

Night-time comes
   with children washing

Night-time comes
   with adults relaxing

Night-time comes
   with tea burning

Night-time comes
   with people nibbling

Night-time comes
   with stars glistening

Night-time comes
   with people snoring

Night-time comes
   with doors slamming

Night-times comes
   with the moon sparkling

Night-time comes
   with everyone sleeping.

Jenna Maria Dingle (9)
St Mary's CE Primary School, Truro

Night-Time
(Based on 'Morning' by Grace Nichols)

Night-time comes
With fire gleaming

Night-time comes
With a bubble bath so relaxing

Night-time comes
With moonlight shining

Night-time comes
With every owl twittering

Night-time comes
With fat sizzling

Night-time comes
With dads snoring

Night-time comes
With babies crying

Night-time comes
With wolves howling

Night-time comes to drag me to bed
Bossy old night-time.

Matthew Cook (10)
St Mary's CE Primary School, Truro

Night
(Based on 'Morning' by Grace Nichols)

Night comes
  with trees moaning.

Night comes
  with the fire crackling.

Night comes
  with the loud owls hooting.

Night comes
  with my little brother yawning.

Night comes
  with the stars shimmering.

Night comes
  with the chips frying.

Night comes
  with TV watching.

Night comes
  with my lights flickering.

Night ends
  with me sleeping.

Thomas Bryant (10)
St Mary's CE Primary School, Truro

Night Comes
(Based on 'Morning' by Grace Nichols)

Night comes
 with the moon twinkling

Night comes
 with the stars flickering

Night comes
 with the trees swishing

Night comes
 with the butter melting

Night comes
 with mum cooking

Night comes
 with spider webs glistening

Night comes
 with owls hooting

Night comes
 with Dad snoring

Night comes to drag me into bed
Boss-woman-night.

Elliot Powell
St Mary's CE Primary School, Truro

Night Comes
(Based on 'Morning' by Grace Nichols)

Night comes
with my dad snoring

Night comes
with my mum working

Night comes
with houses burning

Night comes
when we're eating

Night comes
with the bell ringing

Night comes
with people singing

Night comes
with people moaning

Night comes
with people listening

Night comes with people dragging me into bed
Bossy woman warning.

Holly Manley (9)
St Mary's CE Primary School, Truro

Glistening Night
(Based on 'Morning' by Grace Nichols)

Night comes
with it first beginning

Night comes
with stars gleaming

Night comes
with cats purring

Night comes
with my dad snoring

Night comes
with my milk pouring

Night comes
with the leaves blowing

Night comes
with me dreaming

Night comes
when day is just ending.

Lauren Jones (9)
St Mary's CE Primary School, Truro

Evening
(Based on 'Morning' by Grace Nichols)

Evening comes
With cars vroom vrooming

Evening comes
With street lights flickering

Evening comes
With mum's nagging

Evening comes
With chips cooking

Evening comes
With the TV blaring

Evening comes
With my mum's partner snoring

Evening comes
With my dog barking

Evening comes
With owls whistling

Evening comes
With trees groaning.

Stephen Timms (9)
St Mary's CE Primary School, Truro

Night
(Based on 'Morning' by Grace Nichols)

Night comes
With stars twinkling

Night comes
With moon sparkling

Night comes
With bed creaking

Night comes
With children sleeping

Night comes
With owls hooting

Night comes
With fire burning

Night comes
With clocks ticking

Night comes
With Dad snoring

Night comes to take me to bed
Boss woman night.

Joshua Collett (10)
St Mary's CE Primary School, Truro

Afternoon Comes
(Based on 'Morning' by Grace Nichols)

Afternoon comes
with food steaming

Afternoon comes
with the sun shining

Afternoon comes
with children shouting

Afternoon comes
with parents relaxing

Afternoon comes
with children working

Afternoon comes
with parents shopping

Afternoon comes
with trees swaying

Afternoon comes
with people drinking

Afternoon comes
with children packing.

Jake Rostill (9)
St Mary's CE Primary School, Truro

Night-Times
(Based on 'Morning' by Grace Nichols)

Night comes
The stars are flashing

Night comes
With babies crying

Night comes
Hot bath waiting

Night comes
Trees swishing

Night comes
7 o'clock is coming

Night comes
The moon is shining

Night comes
Rain is dripping

Night comes
Washing is flapping.

Aiden Franklin (9)
St Mary's CE Primary School, Truro

Night Comes
(Based on 'Morning' by Grace Nichols)

Night comes
With the stars glinting

Night comes
With the moon glistening

Night comes
With the fire crackling

Night comes
With people snoring

Night comes
With owls hooting

Night comes
With a wolf howling

Night comes
With the alarm setting
And your pillow is waiting.

Isaac Sutcliffe (9)
St Mary's CE Primary School, Truro

Night-Time
(Based on 'Morning' by Grace Nichols)

Night-time comes
With television watching

Night-time comes
With stars twinkling

Night-time comes
With owls hooting

Night-time comes
With adults drinking

Night-time comes
With children playing

Night-time comes
With parents resting

Night-time comes
With teeth brushing

Night-time comes
With Dad snoring

Night-time comes to drag me into bed
With me sleeping.

Alexander Driver (10)
St Mary's CE Primary School, Truro

Night
(Based on 'Morning' by Grace Nichols)

Night comes
With owls hooting

Night comes
With stars twinkling

Night comes
With the moon shining

Night comes
With the wind whistling

Night comes
With my dad snoring

Night comes
With the TV chattering

Night comes
With my mum cooking

Night comes
With children sleeping

Night comes
With the sea swishing

Night comes
To put me into bed.

Rebecca Gorman (9)
St Mary's CE Primary School, Truro

Lunchtime
(Based on 'Morning' by Grace Nichols)

Lunchtime comes
With the bell ringing

Lunchtime comes
With children playing

Lunchtime comes
With people shouting

Lunchtime comes
With money jingling

Lunchtime comes
With people eating

Lunchtime comes
With lips licking

Lunchtime comes
With tongues clacking

Lunchtime comes
With lots of burping

Lunchtime ends
With Miss Brown teaching.

Jacob De La Mare (10)
St Mary's CE Primary School, Truro

Night
(Based on 'Morning' by Grace Nichols)

Night comes
When the dark is coming

Night comes
When the owls are singing

Night comes
When your dad is snoring

Night comes
When the doors are creaking

Night comes
When the moon is lighting

Night comes
When the dogs are howling

Night comes
When the clock is tick-tocking

Night comes
When the children are moaning.

Night comes to make me stare.

Lewis Jones (10)
St Mary's CE Primary School, Truro

Night

(Based on 'Morning' by Grace Nichols)

Night comes
when my eyes keep closing

Night comes
when everyone comes home from drinking

Night comes
when we start sleeping

Night comes
when I start sleeping

Night comes
when the stars start twinkling

Night comes
when people start sleeping

Night comes
when the night animals start playing

Night comes
when the trains stop

Night comes
to drag me into bed.

William Perry (10)
St Mary's CE Primary School, Truro

Lunchtime Comes
(Based on 'Morning' by Grace Nichols)

Lunchtime comes
when people's tummies are rumbling

Lunchtime comes
when everyone's eating

Lunchtime comes
with people giggling

Lunchtime comes
with people fighting

Lunchtime comes
with people playing

Lunchtime comes
with people screaming

Lunchtime comes
with people talking

Lunchtime comes
with people running

Lunchtime comes to drag me to the table
and to Boss woman land.

Ross Whyte (10)
St Mary's CE Primary School, Truro

Night Comes
(Based on 'Morning' by Grace Nichols)

Night comes
when the stars are twinkling

Night comes
when the moon is beaming

Night comes
when children are sleeping

Night comes
when people are eating

Night comes
when the fire is gleaming

Night comes
when the bed springs are curling

Night comes
when the sun goes down

Night comes
when everyone is in bed.
Boss woman night!

Courtney Rose Cavanagh (10)
St Mary's CE Primary School, Truro

Night
(Based on 'Morning' by Grace Nichols)

Night comes
when the cat is creeping

Night comes
when the owl is hooting

Night comes
when your dad is snoring

Night comes
when the stars are shining

Night comes
when the moon is brightening

Night comes
when the mouse is moving

Night comes
when the wolf is howling.

Night comes
when your mum is cooking

Night comes
before the morning!

Kai Hankins (9)
St Mary's CE Primary School, Truro

Jabbermockery

(Based on 'Jabberwocky' by Lewis Carroll)

'Twas Monday and the cheeky kids,
Did eat and mumble in the hall
All mimsy was the dinner-witches
And the food was grim.

'Beware the dinner-man, my friend!
His food that kills, his spoons that catch!
Beware the lunch-eels and eat
The evil earring snatch.'

He took the bended fork in hand
Long time the problem's end, he sought
So rested by the school canteen
And sat awhile in thought.

And in toughish thought, he sat
The dinner-witch with eyes of flame
Came charging through the lunch room doors
And swallowed as she came.

She thought real fast as we went past
The well placed soap went slickersnack!
She left them stunned and with the rum
She went galumping back!

'And has thou got the answer boy?
Come to my desk,' beamed dinner-man.
'Oh fabulous day, quelle heure Calais!'
They sobbed in their sadness.

'Twas Monday and the cheeky kids,
Did eat and mumble in the hall
All mimsy was the dinner-witches
And the food was grim.

Shannon Bickham (10)
Threemilestone School

Jabbermockery
(Based on 'Jabberwocky' by Lewis Carroll)

'Twas Tuesday and linner dadies
Did gyre and gimble in the lunchin' hall,
All mimsy was Miss Horrogrove,
And everyone was grim.

Beware the carouts and stread, my friend,
And the knife that smacks and the eggs that are hatched,
Beware the burnt bird and shun
The evil money snatch.

She took her bent ladle in hand,
Long time the problem's end she sought,
So rested by the oven
And cooked slop awhile in thought.

And in sloppish thought she sat
The head teacher with eyes of flame,
Came waving her finger down the hall,
And shouted as she came.

She thought real fast as the Head went past;
The well placed skusurd went slipersmack!
She left her stunned
And with her ladle went galumping back.

'And has thou got the answers dinner lady?
Come to my office,' smiled the Head.
'Oh let me think the sack for you, quelle heure Calais!'
Head sniggered with joy.

'Twas Tuesday and the linner dadies
Did gyre and gimble in the lunchin' hall
All mimsy was Miss Horrorgrove
And everyone was grim.

Odette Smaldon (11)
Threemilestone School

Jabbermockery
(Based on 'Jabberwocky' by Lewis Carroll)

'Twas Monday and the stupid girls
Did sit and scratch their heads
All angrout was Mr Detention
And the helper, she was red

Beware the maths man, my friend
His sumcalats are tricky and conard
Beware the quizets, terrible
The evil marking pen

She took her pencil in hand
The problems went snickersmak!
So she ran down to the lavatory
And sat awhile in thought

And as in roughish thought she sat
The maths man with eyes of sums
Came adding down the corridor
And shouted as he ran

She thought real fast as he came past
She tripped him up, bang crash!
She left him stunned to find answers
Galumping back

'And has though passed the quizet Jackie
Come to my arms, clever girl
Oh frabious day coolah coohlay.'
The mum chortled in her joy

'Twas Monday and the stupid girls
Did sit and scratch their heads
All angrout was Mr Detention
And the helper, she was red.

Elaine Dyer (11)
Threemilestone School

Jabberdinnery

(Based on 'Jabberwocky' by Lewis Carroll)

'Twas Friday and the giggly girls,
Did gyre and gimble in the hall,
All flimsy was Miss Rockerbye,
And Mr Chris was tall.

Beware the dinner lady, my friend!
Her forks that snarl, her knives that catch,
The evil penny snatch.

She took her knife and fork in hand,
Long time the horrid food she ate,
So off she went with her friends
And started to debate.

And as in toughish thought they sat,
The dinner lady with eyes of flame.
Came serving through the dinner hall doors
And laughed as she came.

She thought real fast as she went past,
The well placed peas went mushlumpy!
She left her stunned and with the grub,
She went halooting back.

'And have you got the food, Jackie?
Come to our desk,' beamed greedy boys.
'Oh fraberous funilled quelle heure Calais!'
They chortled in their joy.

'Twas Friday and the giggly girls,
Did gyre and gimble in the hall,
All flimsy was Miss Rockerbye,
And Mr Chris was tall.

Laura Barr (11)
Threemilestone School

The Jabbermockery
(Based on 'Jabberwocky' by Lewis Carroll)

'Twas lunchtime and the ringing bell,
Did ding and dong in the school.
All tired was Miss Trelakell,
And the ice cream was cool.

Beware the dinner ladies, so shun,
Their cookers that roast, their fridges that freeze.
Beware the spoons and forks and run,
From the evil roasting pork.

He took his lucky pencil in hand;
Long time the problems middle he sought -
So rested he by the baking tree,
And sat awhile in thought.

And as in hungry thought he sat
The dinner ladies with eyes of cake
Came frying over the canteen mat,
And ate pizza as they came.

He thought real fast as they went past;
The well placed peas went sloppersmack!
He left them stunned and with the buns
He went a running back.

'And has thou got the cookies Acshay?
Come to our table,' beamed the boys.
'Oh frabjous day, Callooh! Callay!'
They chortled in their joy.

'Twas lunchtime and the ringing bell
Did ding and dong in the school.
All tired was Miss Trelakell,
And the ice cream was cool.

Adam M Jarvis (10)
Threemilestone School

The Jabberkitty
(Based on 'Jabberwocky' by Lewis Carroll)

'Twas Monday and the kitty kat
Did gyre and gimble and they sat,
All mimsy was Miss Kataknow,
    And Mr Tom was thin.

'Beware the English, Kat my friend!
His sentence that snarls, his paragraphs that catch.
Beware the Deputy Mouse and shun
    The evil squeaking Tun.'

She took her birdy pen in hand,
Long time till the sentence stands.
So rested she by a science lab,
    And sat awhile in thought.

And in kuttufish thought, she sat,
The English kat with eyes of flame,
Came writing through the cloakroom doors
    And stamping as he came.

She thought real fast as he went past,
The well placed teabag went smickersmack!
She left him, turned and with the sentence
    She went galumping back.

'And has thou got the answer, Kathy?'
'Come to my desk,' beamed a little kat.
'Oh frabish day quelle heure! Salmons.'
    They jumped in their joy.

'Twas Monday and the kitty kat
Did gyre and gimble and they sat,
All mimsy was Miss Kataknow,
    And Mr Tom was thin.

Kenza Thompson-Hewitt (10)
Threemilestone School

Jabermockery
(Based on 'Jabberwocky' by Lewis Carroll)

'Twas Monday and the naughty boys,
Did gyre and gimble in the loo,
All mimsy was Miss Factmes,
And Mr Math had flu.

Beware the Calculsum Man, my friend!
His tests that snarl. Beware his adake,
Beware the Deputy Bird and shun
The evil add 'n' take.

He took his sharp-tipped pencil in hand,
Long time the test end he sought -
So rested he beside the door,
And stood awhile in thought.

And as in confusion thought, he sat,
The Calculsum Man with eyes of flame,
Came thinking through the classroom door
And dividing as he came.

He thought real fast as he flew past;
The well placed ruler went slipertyslap!
He left him amazed and with the test
He went galumping back.

'And has thou got the test Jack?'
'Run to the desk,' beamed jealous boys,
'Oh wonderful day, Quelle heure! Calais!'
They chortled in their joy.

'Twas Monday and the naughty boys,
Did gyre and gimble in the loo,
All mimsy was Miss Factmes,
And Mr Maths had flu.

Emily McConville (11)
Threemilestone School

Jabbermockery
(Based on 'Jabberwocky' by Lewis Carroll)

'Twas Friday and the clever girls
Did gyre and gimble in DT,
All silly was Miss Designaoak
And grim was Miss Technology.

Beware the letter, Man my friend!
His words that snarl, his stories that catch.
Beware the Deputy Bird and shun
The evil earring-snatch.

She took her corex gun in hand;
Long time the problem's end, she sought -
So rested she by the DT door
And sat awhile in thought.

And in toughish thought she sat,
The Letter Man with eyes of flame.
Came stamping through the cloakroom doors
And was writing as he came.

She was real fast as he went past,
The well shot corex went slikersmack!
She left him stunned and with the word
She went runalopping back.

'And have you got the 'ue pot Sophie?'
'Come to my desk,' beamed the idle boy.
'Oh fabjuos day. Hip hip hoorah!'
They chortled in their joy.

'Twas Friday and the clever girls,
Did gyre and gimble in DT.
All silly was Miss Designaoak
And grim was Miss Technology.

Heidi Carthew (10)
Threemilestone School

Jabberdinnery

(Based on 'Jabberwocky' by Lewis Carroll)

'Twas Tuesday lunch and the dinner lady
Did gyre and gimble in the canteen
All mimsy was Miss Boringrove
And Mr Supervisor was grim

Beware the dinner lady, my pupil
The spatulas that smack, the tongs that catch
Beware the head bird and shun
The evil vice captain boy

He took his fork in hand
Long time nice food he sought
So rested he by the boys' lavatory
And sat awhile in no thought

And as in no thought, he sat
The dinner lady with eyes of flame
Came splurging through the lavatory doors
Flinging food as she came

He thought real fast as she went past
The well placed roller skate went slickersmack!
He left her stunned and with the spatula
He went galumping back

'And has thou stunned the dinner lady?'
'Come to my desk, beamed Mr Gone-off Milk
'Oh frabjous day hooray - hooray!'
He chortled in his joy.

'Twas Tuesday and the new dinner lady
Did gyre and gimble in the canteen
All mimsy was Miss Boringrove
and Mr Supervisor wasn't grim.

Joseph Varker (10)
Threemilestone School

Yellow

Yellow is the smell of sunflowers
Yellow is the hot sun
Yellow is the glow of the sun
Warm yellow sand on the beach
Yellow is light like smooth bed sheets.

Katie Parkin (9)
Werrington CP School

Grey

Grey makes me scared in the forest,
Grey is being in a cold home.
Grey is the clouds bashing together,
Grey is the tree in the distance.
Grey is a scary feeling,
Grey is the mist on the moors.

Shannon Sargent (9)
Werrington CP School

Red

Red is ketchup,
Red is blood in the hospital.
Hot scalding water,
Red is bright apples,
Red is heavy,
Red is a sign of danger.

Sam Wooldridge (9)
Werrington CP School

Purple

Purple is loud, heavy and hot,
Purple are horrible olives.
Purple is thunder going boom.
Purple is food colouring in pastry,
Purple are plums, sour and tasty,
Purple are robes and jewels.
Purple is a heart, going boom, boom!
Purple is my headache, saying bang!
Purple are the veins in my body.

Danielle Stearn (9)
Werrington CP School

White

White is cold, like the lick of an ice cream,
White is a frozen icy stream.
White are raindrops falling on the ground,
White is light and a nice quiet sound,
White is free, careful and happy.
White is a nice old carefree chappy,
White is a blizzard under the sea,
White are clouds, far away, I can see.
White is the sparkle of the morning clouds.
White is the very opposite of loud.
White is deep down, inside you.
White is the same as snow too.
White are the answers that I know,
White is the ball that people throw.
White is paper which I write on,
White is the board that I learn on.

Alice Hopkins (8)
Werrington CP School

Green

Green is a sweet crunchy apple,
Green is the sound of leaves blowing,
Green is feeling happy
Green is the forest trees, rustling.

Mark Gribble (7)
Werrington CP School

Red Is . . .

Red is the sun burning my skin,
Red is as juicy as an apple.
Red is danger in my nightmare.
Red is the rustling of the leaves in autumn.
Red is the smell of flowers.

Dean Parkin (7)
Werrington CP School

Blue

Blue is the roaring waves smashing on the slippery stones,
Blue is the tide at high water level.
Blue is the calm and gentle sky.
Blue is the fish swimming in the deep gullies.

Harry Gilbert (8)
Werrington CP School